THE SIS

Listening devices inside a telephone handset

THE SIS

ODYSSEYS

KRISSY EBERTH

CREATIVE EDUCATION · CREATIVE PAPERBACKS

Published by Creative Education and Creative Paperbacks
P.O. Box 227, Mankato, Minnesota 56002
Creative Education and Creative Paperbacks
are imprints of The Creative Company
www.thecreativecompany.us

Design and production by Graham Morgan
Art direction by Tom Morgan
Edited by Jill Kalz

Images by Getty Images/AFP, 44, Arthur Schatz, 2, Bloomberg, 52, Central Press, 25, 30–31, 63 (top), Greg Williams, 22, Historical, 18, Howard Pugh (Marais), cover, Keystone, 26, Margaret Bourke-White, 11, MASTER, 43, Paul Popper/Popperfoto, 60, Popperfoto, 63 (bottom), UniversalImagesGroup, 8, 17, Wathiq Khuzaie, 66–67; INA FASSBENDER/Reuters, 40; Pexels/ready made, 49, Thibault Luycx, 59; Unsplash/Natallia Nagorniak, 35; Wikimedia Commons/Carl Van Vechten, 55, Garry Knight, 75, MI6, 37, Military Intelligence, 6, Nehemia Gershuni-Aylho, 72, public domain, 12, 50, 71, Rama, 4–5

Every effort has been made to contact copyright holders for material reproduced in this book. Any omissions will be rectified in subsequent printings if notice is given to the publisher.

Copyright © 2025 Creative Education, Creative Paperbacks
International copyright reserved in all countries. No part of this book may be reproduced in any form without written permission from the publisher.

Library of Congress Cataloging-in-Publication Data
Names: Eberth, Krissy, author.
Title: The SIS / Krissy Eberth.
Description: Mankato, MN : Creative Education and Creative Paperbacks, [2025] | Series: Odysseys in spycraft | Includes bibliographical references and index. | Audience: Ages 12–15 | Audience: Grades 7–9 | Summary: "Unlock the spy secrets of the United Kingdom's Secret Intelligence Service (SIS; also, MI6), from the British espionage agency's history to counterterrorism training and key missions. Includes a glossary, sidebars, index, and further resources"—Provided by publisher.
Identifiers: LCCN 2024018504 (print) | LCCN 2024018505 (ebook) | ISBN 9798889892922 (library binding) | ISBN 9781682776582 (paperback) | ISBN 9798889894032 (ebook)
Subjects: LCSH: Intelligence service—Great Britain. | Espionage—Great Britain.
Classification: LCC JN329.I6 E24 2025 (print) | LCC JN329.I6 (ebook) | DDC 327.1241—dc23/eng/20240513
LC record available at https://lccn.loc.gov/2024018504
LC ebook record available at https://lccn.loc.gov/2024018505

Printed in the United States of America

Official coat of arms of the United Kingdom of Great Britain and Northern Ireland

CONTENTS

Introduction 9
Founding and Origins 13
   A Killing Code 17
   Code-Breakers 18
What It Takes to Spy 23
   Operation Cupcake 35
Tools and Tricks 36
   Facebook Faux Pas 49
Notable Agents 51
   Quite the HQ 52
   Counting Cigars 59
On a Mission 61
   Plotting in Iraq 66
Selected Bibliography 76
Glossary 77
Websites 79
Index 80

Introduction

In 1588, a powerful fleet of ships sailed north from Spain, intent on destroying the English navy and conquering England. The Spanish might have succeeded if their attack had been a surprise. Instead, a spy planted inside the Spanish king's court by the English secretary of state relayed vital **intelligence** about the attack. Thanks to that advance warning, the English navy was able to defeat the Spanish Armada.

OPPOSITE: After successfully battling the Spanish fleet, England's fortunes increased around the world, and Spain's declined.

English rulers and government leaders from Queen Elizabeth I (1533–1603) to Queen Victoria (1819–1901) often used spies both inside and outside the country. Yet Great Britain did not have an official intelligence organization until 1909. That was the year that the Secret Service Bureau was established. It consisted of two main components: a Foreign Section to handle intelligence gathering and **covert** operations outside the country and a Home Section responsible for catching spies and fighting terrorism domestically.

The more formal name of Secret Intelligence Service (SIS) was adopted for the Foreign Section in 1922. Although officially still known as the SIS, the agency has gone by many different names throughout the years, including Foreign Intelligence Service, Secret Service, MI1(c), Special Intelligence Service, and MI6, which is short for Military Intelligence Section 6.

Great Britain's Royal Air Force and the SIS documented bombing sites and gathered intelligence in the 1940s.

Founding and Origins

The first head of Great Britain's Secret Service Bureau was Captain Mansfield Cumming, who served from 1909 until his death in 1923. Cumming instituted several traditions that continue today. For example, he always signed his name with the initial "C." The letter stood for both "Cumming" and "Chief." All SIS chiefs since Cumming have also been called "C," no matter what their name has been. (In Ian Fleming's famous James Bond British spy novels, the head of the SIS is similarly known as "M.")

OPPOSITE: Sir Mansfield Cumming always used green ink for writing notes, and a bottle of it still sits atop the SIS chief's desk in London today.

Cumming enforced a culture of strict secrecy on the SIS. Agents' names were never publicly revealed, not even if they died in service. Agents were also prohibited from telling others anything about their training, colleagues, or missions. That ban is still in effect today. In fact, revealing agency secrets is against British law, as one former agent, Richard Tomlinson, unfortunately discovered. Tomlinson was imprisoned in the late 1990s when he tried to publish a memoir of his experiences. (He later succeeded in his goal, thanks in large part to the Internet.)

Just five years after the Secret Service Bureau was formed, Europe entered World War I (1914–18). The Foreign Section (later called the SIS) joined with intelligence organizations from France, Italy, Russia, and the United States to monitor the movement of Germany's troops during the war. It also established its first foreign offices in the Netherlands, France, Egypt, and the United States. The Home Section, meanwhile, focused on uncovering German spies operating inside England. Even though the Home Section had only 14 employees at the time, it managed to identify and break up several active German **spy rings**. Its greatest triumph occurred on August 4, 1914, the same day that Great Britain declared war on Germany, when British agents captured 21 German spies they had been tracking.

Following World War I, British intelligence focused on threats to Europe from **communist** Russia, where a political and social revolution had taken place. Russia's new leaders had renamed their country the Soviet Union. Fearing that these leaders were planning to spread communism throughout Europe, the SIS sent two top agents into the Soviet Union. The agents hoped to kill Vladimir Lenin, the leader of the communist revolution, but they were unsuccessful.

Paying so much attention to the Soviet Union distracted British intelligence from Adolf Hitler's rise to power within Germany's Nazi Party in the 1930s. As World War II (1939–45) loomed, two new organizations were established under SIS control. One was the Government Code and Cypher School (GC&CS), based at Bletchley Park near London. Its original objectives were to help

A Killing Code

Because Queen Elizabeth I (1558–1603) was Protestant, many European leaders who were Catholic wanted to overthrow her. She appointed Sir Francis Walsingham as her secretary of state. Walsingham **recruited** and trained a group of college students to become spies, teaching them how to break codes and do undercover work. One time, Walsingham's spies learned of a plot to kill Elizabeth and put her Catholic cousin Mary, Queen of Scots, on the throne. They intercepted and decoded the message from Mary herself to one of the conspirators. The evidence of Mary's guilt led Elizabeth to order her cousin's execution.

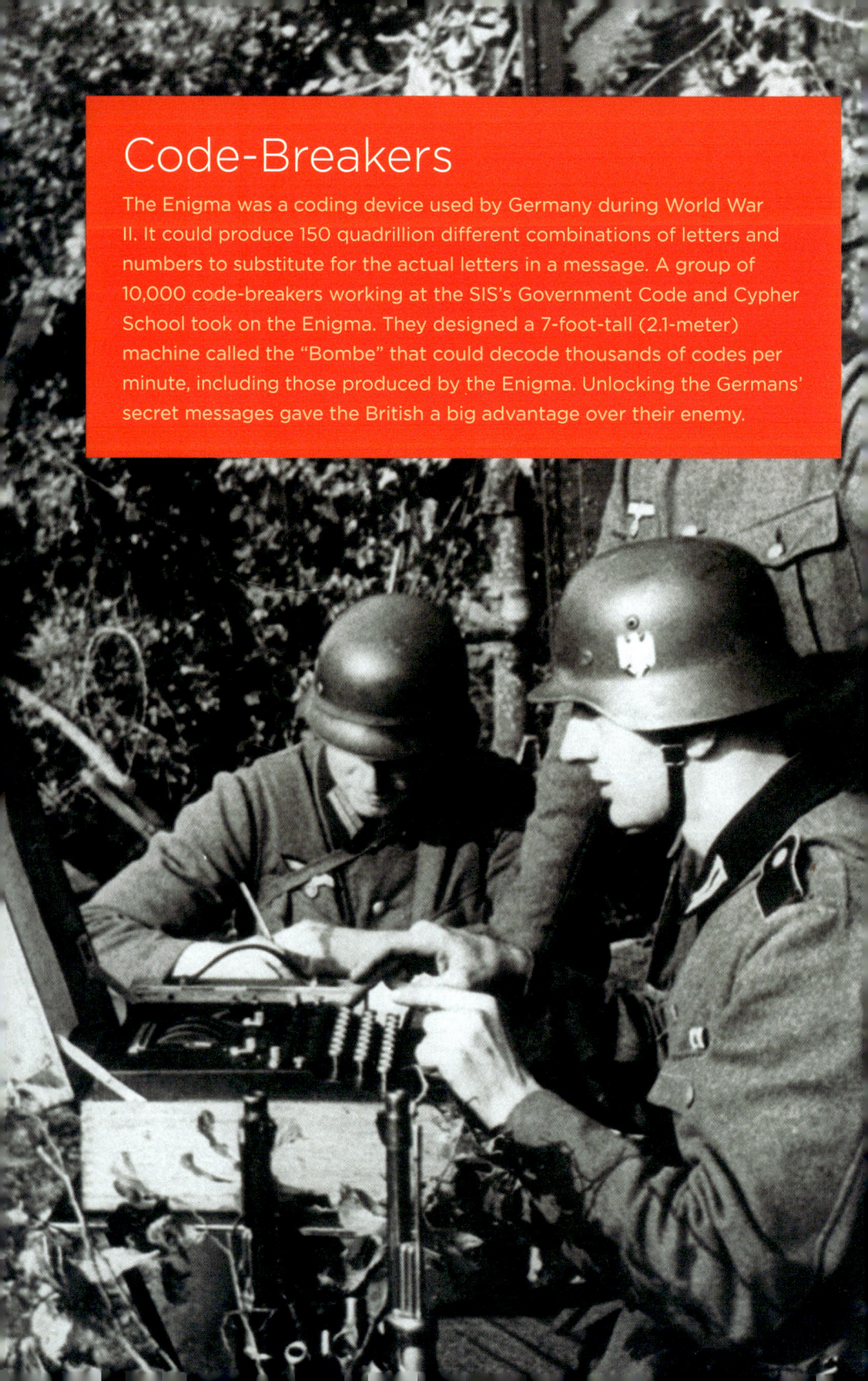

Code-Breakers

The Enigma was a coding device used by Germany during World War II. It could produce 150 quadrillion different combinations of letters and numbers to substitute for the actual letters in a message. A group of 10,000 code-breakers working at the SIS's Government Code and Cypher School took on the Enigma. They designed a 7-foot-tall (2.1-meter) machine called the "Bombe" that could decode thousands of codes per minute, including those produced by the Enigma. Unlocking the Germans' secret messages gave the British a big advantage over their enemy.

break the complex Enigma communications codes used by the Germans and to relay disinformation. The second organization was the Special Operations Executive (SOE), founded in 1940 to carry out **sabotage** behind enemy lines and help resistance groups operating in countries occupied, or controlled, by Germany. Many amazing missions were carried out by SOE agents.

After World War II ended, a new type of conflict called the **Cold War** (1945–91) began. On one side was the United States and its allies, including Great Britain. On the other side was the Soviet Union and its allies in Eastern Europe. During the Cold War, the SIS joined with the Central Intelligence Agency (CIA) in the United States in several operations to undermine the KGB, the main Soviet intelligence agency. For example, during the 1960s, SIS agents managed to recruit several important

KGB agents as **double agents**. At the same time, though, it was discovered that key SIS leaders had been selling British and American secrets to the Soviets.

The budget for Great Britain's spy work was severely slashed during the 1970s, and the agency shrank in size. Then Margaret Thatcher was elected prime minister in 1979, and, as the government's leader, she made **espionage** an important part of her foreign policy throughout the next decade. The staff of the SIS was expanded to include more than 2,000 employees dur-

"SINCE THE END OF THE COLD WAR … THE SIS HAS CONCENTRATED ON COMBATING TERRORISM."

ing that time. In 2021, that number had risen to 3,600, although exact numbers are always kept secret.

Since the end of the Cold War and breakup of the Soviet Union in 1991, the SIS has concentrated on combating terrorism, particularly in the Middle East. British espionage efforts have been directed toward uncovering the secrets related to conflict and war in countries such as Afghanistan, Ukraine, Zimbabwe, and Israel. SIS has also had to focus its attention on thwarting bombings or other types of attack such as those made on the London public transit system in 2005. Ever-changing threats of all kinds have required British intelligence agencies to update and retool their methods of spying for the 21st century.

THE SIS

What It Takes to Spy

Because of fictional characters such as James Bond (Agent 007), many people think spies need to be handsome/beautiful, daring, and a little conceited. Not surprisingly, novels, movies, and TV shows exaggerate reality to provide engaging entertainment. SIS agents are certainly expected to be smart, resourceful, and self-reliant, like 007, but being average-looking is just fine. In fact, people who can blend in with others around them, who don't stand out in a crowd, make the best spies.

OPPOSITE: Actor Daniel Craig has starred as the SIS agent James Bond in five movies—most recently *No Time to Die* (2021).

Fictional spies often lead incredibly exciting lives, filled with nonstop action and danger. They break into impenetrable fortresses and engage in deadly hand-to-hand combat, usually with superhuman results. In real life, only a small percentage of SIS operatives do undercover spy work themselves. These individuals are called case officers. They are often stationed in foreign countries, where they gather intelligence vital to British political, economic, and national security interests. Case officers need to have the ability to "read" others and influence their decision-making. They are central to the SIS's mission. They need to be persuasive and be able to convince others to spy and run the risk of being caught and punished. Sometimes that requires appealing to someone's ego through the use of flattery. Other times, it may call for using blackmail. Some case officers may use top-secret tools and weapons to collect information or to carry out covert actions. Most, however, spend their time talking—recruiting others in the countries where they are stationed and taking on the role of handler.

Assisting the case officers abroad or in Great Britain are two other types of SIS employee: targeting officers and reports officers. Targeting officers need to have excellent

In the 1960s, British reports officers kept a close eye on the Soviet Union's ships in Atlantic waters.

From 1953 to 1961, double agent George Blake shared secrets with the Soviet Union while working for the SIS.

organizational and analytical skills. They are the agents who help plan operations and direct much of what the case officers do. They get their title from the way they keep everything moving smoothly and "on target." For example, they might help select the individuals whom case officers should recruit to do undercover work. They might also pick out locations for **drops** and deliver the intelligence that has been gathered to officials at headquarters.

Reports officers are experts on different countries and subjects. They perform a lot of research and write many reports (which explains their title). Reports officers test the intelligence to make sure it is sound. They are responsible for distributing intelligence reports from the field to government leaders who need to know the information, and they often represent the SIS at meetings with other government organizations on specific topics.

Reports officers spend most of their time in Great Britain, even when their minds are traveling to foreign locations.

To survive in the field, an SIS case officer needs a good **legend**. The legend answers the questions "Who am I?" and "What am I doing here?" Some case officers work under their own names. In spy talk, they are legals—they do their spying and recruitment while officially working in the British embassy in a foreign country or in a British-owned business. If they are caught breaking the foreign country's law, they are usually sent back to England rather than jailed.

Other case officers are classified as illegals—they work under a false name and a made-up identity. Sometimes their legends are very detailed and complex. For example, the SIS may create a fake business in which some employees are illegals. The business serves as a front for collecting intelligence and relaying it back to headquarters. If illegals are exposed as spies, they often face stiff prison sentences—or worse.

With all the risks involved, what makes people want to be spies—or agree to become spies against their will? The reasons are different for every agent. Some people are looking for adventure. Others want to serve the country they love. Spy work is challenging and constantly changing, yet it is often dangerous. "It is also quite glamorous," said one SIS agent who was interviewed on a British radio program. "You might find yourself on one day in a tent talking to tribal

Some people become spies because they're risk-takers, willing to put themselves in harm's way to meet a challenge.

leaders in the middle of nowhere and 24 hours later be in a different country talking to a high-powered financier."

Citizens of other countries may have different explanations for why they spy for the SIS. Some do it because they are paid well for the information they uncover. Others work for the SIS because they feel their home country's government is oppressive or because they have a strong belief in the ideals represented by Great Britain and its allies. Still others may be blackmailed into spying to cover up secret or illegal activities they have engaged in. Individuals who think their wits and courage would best be suited for spying may be drawn to the SIS, too.

In the past, SIS agents were often recruited from major British universities such as Oxford. They were literally tapped on the shoulder by someone connected to the agency who believed they would make good additions to the organization. Today, the SIS does its recruiting via the Internet or by advertising with universities. There is even an online exam that potential recruits can take. One activity involves a test of memory to see whether the potential recruit will be able to establish a legend and remember the details well enough not to slip under questioning.

Once a person is recruited, they might think they have made it into the SIS. However, this is just the beginning. Recruitment is followed by several tough interviews and then a thorough security check. If a potential agent gets that far, the serious training begins and can last for 6 to 18 months. Case officers going into the field need to learn **tradecraft**. These skills include developing a legend and improvising on it as the need arises. They also learn how to avoid being followed. Each agent is trained on how to use spy cameras, radios and detecting devices, and other communication and technological tools. Agents are also trained to mingle comfortably at parties and in the streets without sticking out. Coordinating secret meetings to recruit local **assets** and setting up a drop for collecting intelligence from assets is another type of training that all agents go through. Once they have mastered these skills, recruits are ready to begin their careers as spies and become immersed in a world of secrecy.

Operation Cupcake

In June 2011, SIS agents hacked into computers featuring a downloadable magazine from terrorist group Al-Qaeda. The English-language magazine was designed to encourage terrorist activities in the West. In the cyberattack, the SIS switched out bomb-making instructions, under the heading "Make a Bomb in the Kitchen of Your Mom," with something sweeter. Instead of receiving instructions for making an explosive, readers got recipes for "The Best Cupcakes in America" from comedian Ellen DeGeneres's TV talk show. While the hack worked, Al-Qaeda was able to correct the switch days later and strengthened their computer security to ensure it wouldn't happen again.

Tools and Tricks

In the 007 movies, British agent James Bond may be the hero, and "M" may be the boss, but the real stars are the amazing gadgets and weapons created by the SIS technical staff led by an officer known as "Q." Whether Bond is driving around in a car that can transform into a submarine, firing nerve gas from a fountain pen, or microfilming secret documents with a camera concealed in a watch, viewers are dazzled by an assortment of spy technology. Even though most of these gadgets are only movie props, real-life SIS agents have had some incredible tools at their disposal created by the agency's technology division.

OPPOSITE: Shoes are a common concealment device for hiding messages, media, drugs, and weapons.

 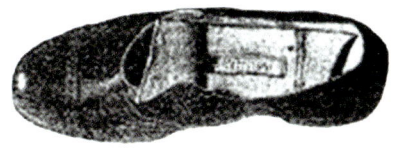

Many of the gadgets developed by SIS technicians are designed to be held in the hands of agents or concealed on their bodies or in their clothing. They fall under the category of HUMINT, or human intelligence tools, because it takes a human to operate such gadgets and collect or send data with them. Two examples that were developed for British agents during World War II were a matchbox with a tiny camera hidden inside and a shaving brush with a secret compartment for storing messages or rolls of microfilm. More modern HUMINT tools employed by case officers include watches with video and audio recording capabilities, cell phones for sending coded messages, night-vision goggles for investigating in the darkness, **bugs** for eavesdropping on conversations or secret meetings, and mini cameras hidden in tie clasps or jacket buttons.

In his controversial 2020 book, *The Big Breach*, former SIS agent Richard Tomlinson, who served from 1991 until his dismissal in 1995, describes several gadgets and communication techniques he was taught to use. One device employed a short-range agent communication (SRAC) system. It allowed an agent to convey brief messages directly to a handler inside a British embassy or other approved location without making face-to face contact or even sending an electronic communication. This cut down on the risk of interception. According to Tomlinson, here is how the SRAC system worked: "The agent writes a message on a laptop computer, then downloads it into the SRAC transmitter, a small box the size of a cigarette packet. The receiver is usually mounted in the British embassy and continually sends out a low-power interrogation signal. When the agent is close enough, in his car or on foot, his transmitter is triggered and transmits the message [which has been converted into high-frequency radio waves]. The transmitter is disguised as a harmless object. For many years 'Garfield Cat' stuffed animals were popular disguises for the transmitter, as their sucker feet allowed the agent to stick the transmitter on the side window of a car, giving an extra clear signal as the agent drove past the embassy."

Tomlinson's training in the early '90s also focused on using special cameras. "We were taught how to take

Early spy cameras could be tough to conceal.

long-range snaps of targets using huge telephoto lenses and how to take clear closeups of documents," Tomlinson said. They also practiced "with gadgets such as tiny cameras and specially made collapsible document-copying cameras. The most fun though, were the lessons on covert photography during which we secretly photographed members of the public with a variety of still and video cameras mounted in briefcases or shoulder bags."

In today's spy world, HUMINT gadgets such as the ones Tomlinson learned to use have taken a back seat to ELINT (electronic intelligence), SIGINT (signal intelligence), and PHOTINT (photographic intelligence) tools. ELINT tools are used for computer monitoring and hacking; SIGINT tools are used for intercepting radio, telephone, and other communications; and PHOTINT tools are used for studying photographs taken by spy planes, satellites, or human operatives. All of these new methods fall under the heading of TECHINT (technical intelligence).

For modern spies, learning to use electronic gadgets has become an important part of their tradecraft. Far less significant is knowing how to handle weapons. In fact, unlike James Bond, many SIS officers seldom use guns, knives, or rocket launchers in their work. Today, it is more important for a spy to know how to hack into a computer than how to engage in hand-to-hand combat. Computers can be bugged with a keystroke recorder that can help an agent determine a user's password and duplicate any commands that were previously typed in. Other software can be installed to enable an agent to download files for later analysis. Most information today is stored and sent digitally, so knowing how to unlock digital files enables a case officer to uncover enemy secrets and, perhaps, prevent an attack.

Computer spying, called cyberespionage, has gotten more sophisticated in recent years.

Surveillance camera images enable the SIS and other British intelligence agencies to prevent crime.

Backing up SIS agents in the use of TECHINT is another British intelligence agency. Known as the Government Communications Headquarters (GCHQ), it was established after World War II as a successor to the GC&CS that broke Germany's Enigma codes. GCHQ carries out many of the same functions as the National Security Agency (NSA) in the United States. More than 7,000 employees use technology to intercept and interpret electronic communications and develop intelligence to combat terrorism and crime in Great Britain. GCHQ also supplies intelligence to British military forces and to SIS agents around the world. Its data is often shared with foreign intelligence agencies such as the CIA, as well.

In an example of cooperative intelligence work, in September 2010, operatives from the SIS and GCHQ, working with CIA agents, used TECHINT tools to

"IN ADDITION TO USING TECHNOLOGY, AGENTS MUST BE ABLE TO DEPLOY TRICKS OF THE TRADE WHEN IN DIFFICULT CIRCUMSTANCES."

thwart a plan to bomb London and several other European capitals. The plot was being developed by terrorists based in England and Pakistan. Intercepted e-mail and phone conversations—as well as **aerial reconnaissance** of terrorist training facilities in Pakistan—helped reveal the plot. British and U.S. leaders acted quickly. Several CIA **drones** flew over parts of northwestern Pakistan, firing missiles to destroy vehicles in which terrorists were riding. Taking out the leaders helped suspend the threat, but European capitals remained on high alert for several days following the drone attack.

In addition to using technology, agents must be able to deploy tricks of the trade when in difficult circumstances. Despite their thorough training, agents can get nervous, and if they misstep, they may not survive. One trick is for agents to use their memory. Former British SIS agent Warren Reed calls this technique the "family home." In this trick, there are two sets of information. The first is the "known," and the second is the "unknown." An agent thinks of a home that they spent a lot of time in or grew up in. This house is the "known" part of the trick. The agent pictures themselves walking around the house and looking at all the rooms, furniture, and decor. Then the agent pictures the "unknown." This is the information they are trying to remember. It may be a conversation they are listening to, the exact shape or color of an object, or a long number. The agent takes this important piece of information and places it in the house somewhere, sometimes in silly ways. For instance, they might envision a double agent squished under the kitchen sink or a password for a computer program in a toilet bowl. The more ridiculous the placement, the easier the information is to remember. Once the agent has placed everything, they walk through their mind's "family home" and see everything in its place and remember. Because unknown elements are paired with well-known elements, they embed easier in the agent's memory. The typical agent can remember 20 items during training. When they use the "family home" method, they can sometimes remember up to 100.

Facebook Faux Pas

Like the rest of the world, today's SIS is embracing technology. The agency even has a presence on social media, including Facebook and Twitter accounts and a website (https://www.sis.gov.uk). But it still needs to maintain a high level of secrecy for security reaons. Social media almost cost Sir John Sawers his job as the SIS chief in 2009. Forgetting to use privacy settings, his wife posted on her Facebook page about their family, including photos, personal interests, their home address, and location of their children. Luckily, the information was removed before anything terrible could happen.

Notable Agents

Robert Baden-Powell, who is best known as the founder of the Scouting Movement (from which the Boy Scouts and Girl Scouts organizations came), was a British spy. In the 1890s, Baden-Powell served as an army intelligence officer reporting on Austria-Hungary, one of Great Britain's enemies at the time. While on assignment, he demonstrated that he was a great actor as well as a spy.

OPPOSITE: Robert Baden-Powell was a member of the British army from 1876 to 1910.

Quite the HQ

Since 1994, the SIS has been headquartered along the River Thames in southwestern London near Vauxhall Bridge. The building has a unique shape. Some SIS employees call it "Legoland" because it looks as if thousands of toy blocks were used to assemble it. No one outside the SIS is sure just what special features the building includes, as such details are top secret. It is rumored, though, that a tunnel under the Thames leads from HQ to British government offices in another part of the city.

On one occasion, Baden-Powell dressed up as a nearsighted butterfly expert exploring the countryside. He made sketch after sketch of insects, adding images of enemy fortifications in the background. These he relayed to British military leaders in the region. On another occasion, Baden-Powell pretended to be a drunken fisherman boating along the Danube River. In that disguise, he was never questioned as to why he was sailing so close to a key Austro-Hungarian fortress. The enemy soldiers even showed Baden-Powell how to operate a new machine gun they were testing!

Several successful British authors have also doubled as spies for the SIS, mostly in wartime. British spymasters reasoned that the well-known writers would not raise enemy suspicions if they appeared in strategic places in Europe, Asia, or Africa. During World War I, novelist W. Somerset Maugham did intelligence work in Europe and was even sent into Russia soon after the 1917 revolution. He was tasked with trying to prevent the communists from making a separate peace treaty with the Germans. After the war, Maugham wrote a collection of stories entitled *Ashenden* based on his intelligence work. Before the collection was published, however, he burned several stories that might have violated the British law.

Another literary spy was children's writer Roald Dahl, later known for books such as *James and the Giant Peach* and *Matilda*. He was a pilot with the Royal Air Force until he sustained serious injuries in a plane crash. Dahl was then assigned to the British Embassy in Washington, D.C. His diplomatic position became a good cover as he worked for the SIS. His mission was to convince U.S. leaders to help European nations in World War II.

Dahl's boss in the United States was William Stephenson, a true intelligence mastermind. British prime

Author Roald Dahl

minister Winston Churchill personally sent the Canadian-born Stephenson to the States in 1940. Stephenson had a dual mission: to keep an eye on German intelligence operations in the United States and to oversee covert operations aimed at getting America to enter the war by whatever means necessary. In 1940, the United States was still a neutral country, and many Americans opposed becoming involved in what they thought was Europe's war. This attitude was known as isolationism.

Stephenson set up an office in midtown New York, established a radio link with London, and chose his new code name, Intrepid. Then he set to work undermining the isolationists. He started by recruiting U.S. journalists, authors, advertising copywriters, and artists to join his operation, which became known as the British Security Coordination (BSC). The journalists helped Stephenson plant stories in newspapers or on the radio to cast the isolationists in a negative light. Well-known authors such as mystery writer Rex Stout wrote pamphlets. Top copywriters and artists created ads that emphasized the evil activities of the Nazis. The pamphlets and ads revealed other secret Nazi "plans" (all untrue) to set up training camps in Mexico for an eventual invasion of the United States. They started rumors that the Nazis planned to replace crosses on European churches with swastikas, the Nazi symbol. Stephenson's campaign scared and angered Americans, and it began to sway them in the direction of helping Great Britain. Still, it was not until Japanese forces attacked American ships at Pearl Harbor on December 7, 1941, that the United States officially joined the Allies in the fight against Germany and Japan.

After Stephenson's main objective was successfully completed, he remained in the United States to run a much smaller SIS station throughout the rest of the war. He also helped his close friend William Donovan establish a civilian intelligence agency called the Office of Strategic Services (OSS). That agency would later evolve into the CIA.

The SIS kept busy during the Cold War, primarily working to turn Soviet agents into double agents or plant moles inside communist intelligence agencies in Russia and other Eastern European countries. One of the most important of these double agents was Oleg Gordievsky, an officer with the KGB, the Russian equivalent of the SIS. In 1973, Gordievsky approached SIS agents and offered to provide them with information about KGB activities and plans. He met more than 150 times with SIS contacts, who took more than 6,000 pages of notes on what proved to be accurate intelligence. Gordievsky also alerted the SIS to the presence of several **traitors** operating inside the agency.

Less than two years later, Gordievsky was himself betrayed by a CIA officer named Aldrich Ames, who was a mole for the Russians. Gordievsky was recalled to the Soviet Union and feared he would be executed. However, SIS agents helped him escape to Great Britain. In the 1980s, he served as an adviser to British prime minister Margaret Thatcher and U.S. president Ronald Reagan.

Counting Cigars

When World War I broke out in 1914, the SIS began searching for spies who might be working in England on behalf of Germany. One case involved a pair of Dutch spies posing as cigar importers. The men would telegraph orders for cigars in code from England to a German contact in the Netherlands. The product type and number of boxes ordered represented the number of different types of ships they saw coming into British ports. Suspicious of the large number of cigars being ordered, British agents arrested the pair, who were later executed for their crime.

THE SIS

On a Mission

One of the most extensive intelligence operations during World War II involved the founding, supplying, and directing of the Special Operations Executive (SOE) between 1940 and 1945, when it was absorbed by the SIS. The SOE was made up of civilians (non-military people) who worked in Nazi-occupied countries such as France, Belgium, Poland, and the Netherlands. In defining its mission, the SOE borrowed a quote from Winston Churchill: "You are to set Europe ablaze!"

OPPOSITE: Some SOE missions during World War II involved agents dropping in behind enemy lines by parachute.

SOE operatives were secretly dropped behind enemy lines, where they set up equipment workshops and radio systems. They sabotaged transportation and power lines, disrupted enemy communications, and destroyed factories supplying arms and equipment for the enemy. SOE agents may not have set Europe on fire, but their efforts did make German military officers angry.

Many of the 3,000 SOE operatives were women without any previous military or intelligence experience. Odette Sansom and Violette Szabo were two well-known SOE agents. Sansom was born in France and moved to England after marrying a British man. In 1942, she volunteered to return to France as a radio operator for the SOE. Around the same time, Szabo, whose husband had been killed in action in North Africa, also joined the SOE. Both women were

Odette Sansom [*center*]

Violette Szabo

later captured by the Germans, tortured, and imprisoned with many other people in concentration camps. Sansom survived the war, but Szabo was executed.

o spy operation during the 20th century was more dramatic or extensive than Operation Bodyguard. The focus of this plan was to deceive Hitler and the German generals on when and where the Allies would invade Europe in 1944. Allied military leaders had already decided to invade at Normandy, France, around June 6, a date known as "D-Day." The objective

of Operation Bodyguard was to persuade the Germans that the invasion would come later and at a different location, such as Pas de Calais, several hundred miles east of Normandy. The operation took its name from another quote by Churchill: "In wartime, truth is so precious that she should always be attended by a bodyguard of lies."

Starting in late 1943, British and U.S. intelligence groups began feeding lies to the Nazi intelligence agency, the Abwehr. Double agents working for the SIS sent reports to Germany about troop buildups in southeastern England. Fake press releases about fictional military units began appearing in magazines and newspapers. A prisoner swap was arranged to return a dying German general to his homeland. First, however, the general was driven past a military camp where he saw hundreds of airplanes, tanks, and tents. The general was told that they

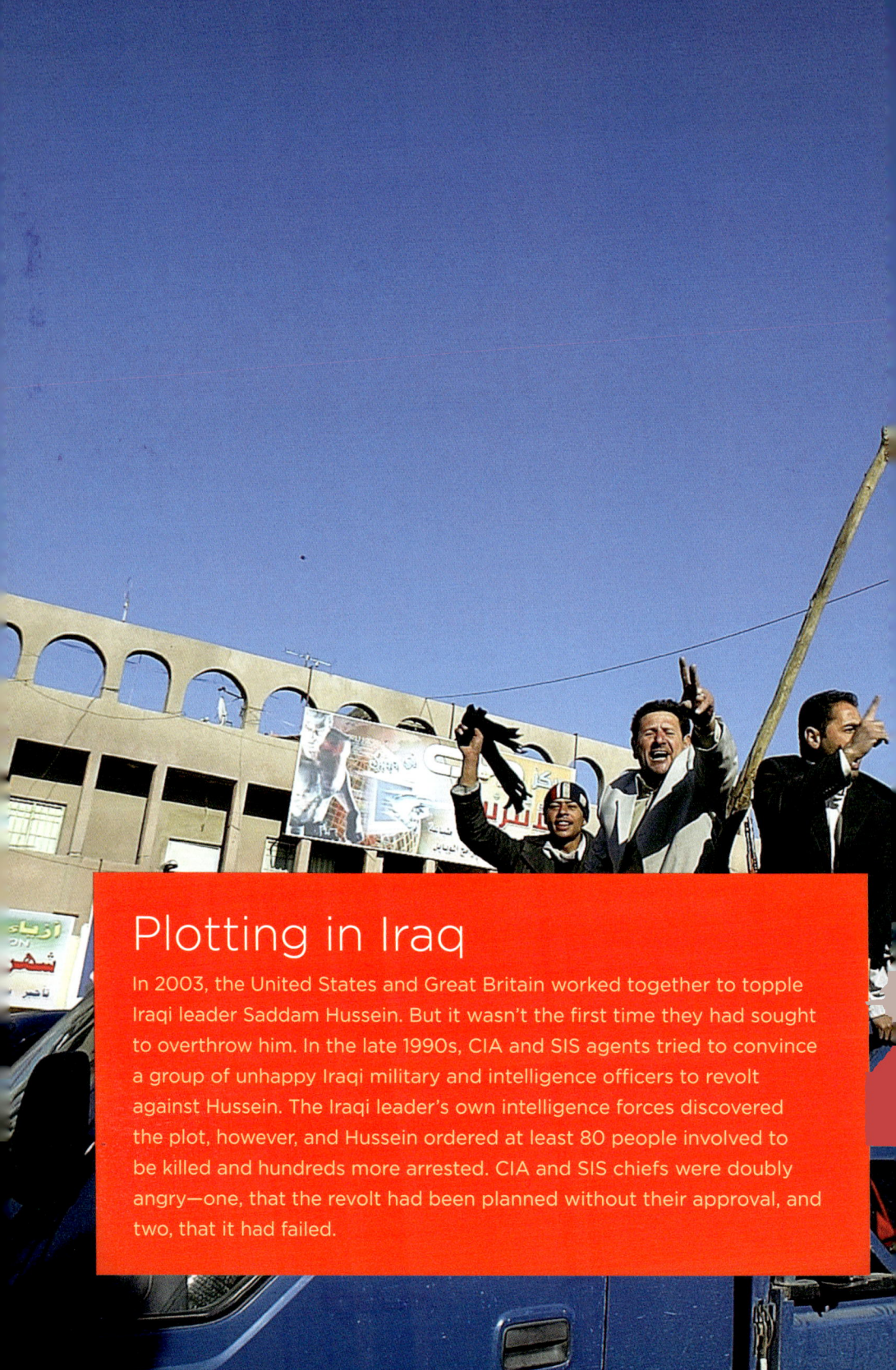

Plotting in Iraq

In 2003, the United States and Great Britain worked together to topple Iraqi leader Saddam Hussein. But it wasn't the first time they had sought to overthrow him. In the late 1990s, CIA and SIS agents tried to convince a group of unhappy Iraqi military and intelligence officers to revolt against Hussein. The Iraqi leader's own intelligence forces discovered the plot, however, and Hussein ordered at least 80 people involved to be killed and hundreds more arrested. CIA and SIS chiefs were doubly angry—one, that the revolt had been planned without their approval, and two, that it had failed.

Iraqi citizens hang a dummy of Saddam Hussein to celebrate his execution in 2006.

were traveling through Sussex, but they were really in Dorset several hundred miles farther west. The Germans became convinced that Pas de Calais was the target, and Hitler directed most of his troops there instead of Normandy. When the Allies struck on D-Day, casualties were great but not nearly on the scale of what they might have been without the disinformation operation.

A decade later, during the Cold War, the SIS suffered through one of its most embarrassing operations. Known as Operation Stopwatch, the 1954 plan involved the construction of a tunnel beneath the Soviet military headquarters in East Berlin. Its purpose was to enable eavesdropping on phone conversations between Germany and the Soviet Union. A similar tunnel had been built in Vienna, Austria, in 1953, and valuable information had been recorded. There was a hitch in the plan for this new tunnel, however. The man responsible for taking notes at SIS planning meetings was operative George Blake, who turned out to be a double agent working for the KGB. Over the next year, British technicians tapped hundreds of phone lines in East Berlin and recorded more than 400,000 conversations. Many of the conversations contained disinformation because the KGB had been alerted by Blake. Then, in 1956, the Soviets "accidentally" discovered the tunnel while doing repair work below their building and shut it down. It would be many years before the SIS learned of Blake's treachery.

During and following the Cold War, the SIS worked closely with the CIA on several key operations. In 1962, for example, the United States was involved in a confrontation with the Soviet Union over Soviet weapons being set up in Cuba, a communist island nation just 90 miles (145 kilometers) from Florida's southern coast. Many people feared that a nuclear war would erupt. Information supplied by the SIS, courtesy of a double agent named Oleg Penkovsky, convinced the Americans that the Soviet weapons were not as powerful as they had originally feared. President John F. Kennedy stood up to Soviet premier Nikita Khrushchev, demanding that the Soviets remove their missiles, and the Soviets backed down.

Oleg Penkovsky [*right*] was tried and executed by the Soviet government as a traitor.

Remotely piloted drones provide intelligence agencies with crucial information.

In the past, threats to British national security were predictable. In today's climate, risks are diverse and always changing. The SIS needs to constantly adapt to fight international terrorism and increased chemical, biological, and nuclear weapon production by groups hostile toward Great Britain. The SIS uses the four Ps: Prevent, Pursue, Protect, and Prepare. It detects and disrupts terrorist plots and threats overseas by partnering with other agencies and allies. It also uses the latest technology to keep the country and its computer networks safe from cyberattacks.

Artificial intelligence (AI) is a new technology that can help the SIS and its allies—but it can also help their enemies. SIS chief Richard Moore commented in a rare speech in July 2023 that British spies had used AI to hinder Russia from obtaining weapons in its war with Ukraine. He also said the SIS was focusing a lot of its attention on China.

Many Western intelligence agencies, such as the CIA and the SIS, worry that they are falling behind China in the AI field. In his speech, Moore insisted that the human factor in the world of intelligence will not be replaced by AI. "As AI trawls the ocean of open source," he said, "there will be even greater value in landing, with a well-cast fly, the secrets that lie beyond the reach of its nets."

While Great Britain's military and political might in the world has declined some in the past century, the innovative nature and scope of its intelligence work have remained strong. The spy agency of James Bond and Mansfield Cumming continues to be involved in exciting missions, both fictitious and factual, and the work of its agents remains vital to world security in the 21st century and beyond. As the agency notes on its website, the SIS prides itself on the ability of its employees to make a difference in the real world.

Some people call the SIS headquarters "Babylon-on-Thames" because it seems to resemble an ancient Babylonian temple.

Selected Bibliography

Bloomberg News. "China Claims It Caught a Foreign Consultant Spying for the U.K.'s MI6." *TIME*. January 8, 2024. https://time.com/6552966/china-foreign-consultant-spy-uk-mi6.

Crowdy, Terry. *The Enemy Within: A History of Espionage.* Oxford; New York: Osprey, 2006.

Dorril, Stephen. *MI6: Inside the Covert World of Her Majesty's Secret Intelligence Service.* New York: Free Press, 2000.

Jeffery, Keith. *The Secret History of MI6*. New York: Penguin Press, 2010.

Lawless, Jill. "Britain's MI6 Chief Says His Spies Are Using AI to Disrupt Flow of Weapons to Russia." The Associated Press. July 19, 2023. https://apnews.com/article/mi6-spy-chief-moore-prague-russia-iran-cfb837ebdfa3db8043dc655cbf3573d5.

Thomas, Gordon. *Secret Wars: One Hundred Years of British Intelligence inside MI5 and MI6.* New York: Thomas Dunne Books, 2009.

Tomlinson, Richard. *The Big Breach: From Top Secret to Maximum Security*. Moscow: Narodny Variant Publishers, 2000.

Glossary

aerial reconnaissance
spying activities conducted through the air using airplanes, balloons, and drones

agent
a person who works for, but is not necessarily officially employed by, an intelligence service

asset
a hidden source acting as a spy or providing secret information to a spy

bug
a hidden recording/listening device

Cold War
the hostile competition between the United States and its allies against the Soviet Union and its allies that began at the end of World War II and lasted until the collapse of the Soviet Union in 1991

communist
related to a political and economic system in which all goods and property are owned by the state and shared by all members of the public

covert
undercover or hidden

double agent
a spy for one country who doubles as a spy for a second country and often provides false information to the first country

drone
an uncrewed aircraft, often directed by remote control, that is used to take secret photographs of or attack targets

drop	a prearranged spot for dropping off and picking up information gathered through spying; also called a dead drop
espionage	the act of spying
intelligence	information uncovered and transmitted by a spy
legend	a cover story
mole	an employee of one intelligence service who actually works for another service or who works undercover in a foreign country to supply intelligence
operative	an undercover agent working for an intelligence agency
recruit	to hire or enlist
sabotage	the act of purposely damaging or destroying something, especially for political or military gain
spy ring	a group or network of spies working together
tradecraft	the procedures, techniques, and devices used by spies to carry out their activities
traitor	a person who betrays another's trust or is false to one's duty or country

Websites

The International Spy Museum
https://www.spymuseum.org
Explore bios of real-life agents and frequently asked questions about spying.

MI6
https://www.britannica.com/topic/MI6
Read a brief history of MI6.

Secret Intelligence Service (MI6)
https://www.sis.gov.uk
Learn more about the SIS directly from its website.

Index

Al-Qaeda, 35
artificial intelligence (AI), 73, 74
Baden-Powell, Robert, 51, 53
Blake, George, 26, 69, 70
Bond, James, 13, 23, 36, 42, 74
British Security Coordination (BSC), 56
China, 73-74
Churchill, Winston, 54, 61, 65
CIA, 19, 45, 57, 58, 70, 74
codes, 17, 18, 19, 37, 45
    Enigma, 18, 19, 45
Cold War, 19, 21, 57, 68, 70
cyberattacks, 35
cyberespionage, 43
Cumming, Mansfield, 13, 14, 74
Dahl, Roald, 54, 55
Donovan, William, 57
double agents, 20, 26, 48, 57, 58, 65, 69, 70
Fleming, Ian, 13
France, 14, 15, 61, 62, 64
Germany, 14, 15, 16, 18, 19, 45, 57, 59, 65, 69
Gordievsky, Oleg, 58
Government Code and Cypher School (GC&CS), 16, 18, 45
Government Communications Headquarters (GCHQ), 45
Hitler, Adolf, 16, 64, 68
Home Section, 10, 15
illegal spies, 29
legal spies, 28
London, England, 16, 46, 52, 56
KGB, 19, 20, 58, 69
Maugham, W. Somerset, 53-54
Moore, Richard, 73, 74
movies and TV shows, 23, 36
Operation Bodyguard, 64-65
Operation Cupcake, 35
Operation Stopwatch, 68-69
Penkovsky, Oleg, 70, 71
Queen Elizabeth I, 10, 17
reasons for spying, 29, 30, 32-33
recruiting, 17, 19, 25, 27, 28, 33, 34, 56

Russia, 14, 15, 53, 57, 73
Sansom, Odette, 62, 63, 64
Sawers, John, 49
Secret Service Bureau, 10, 13, 14
    sections of the, 10
short-range agent communication (SRAC), 38-39
SIS
    alternate names, 10
    chiefs, 13, 49, 66, 73
    headquarters, 27, 29, 52, 75
social media, 49
Soviet Union, 15, 16, 19, 21, 25, 26, 58, 69, 70
Spanish Armada, 9
Special Operations Executive (SOE), 19, 61-62
Stephenson, William, 54-55, 56-57
Stout, Rex, 56
Szabo, Violette, 62, 63, 64
terrorism, 10, 21, 35, 45, 46, 73
Thatcher, Margaret, 20, 58
Tomlinson, Richard, 14, 38, 39, 41
tools of the trade
    bugs, 37
    cameras, 34, 36, 37, 39, 40, 41, 44
    computers, 35, 38, 41, 42, 43
    drones, 46, 47, 72
    "family home" technique, 47-48
    gadgets, 36, 37, 38, 41, 42
    weapons, 25, 36, 42
tradecraft, 34
    legends, 28, 29, 33, 34
training, 34, 38, 39, 47
types of officers
    case, 24-25, 27, 28, 29, 34, 37
    reports, 25, 27, 28
    targeting, 25, 27
United States, 14, 15, 19, 45, 54, 55, 56, 57, 70
Walsingham, Francis, 17
World War I, 14, 15, 53, 59
World War II, 16, 18, 19, 37, 45, 54, 61